The Quotable Cat

The Quotable Cat

*'Cause You Can Never Say
Enough About Them*

Selected by **Denise Little**

**BARNES
& NOBLE
BOOKS**

NEW YORK

2001 Barnes & Noble Books

Text design by Ziga Design

ISBN 0-7607-2364-8

Printed and bound in the United States of America

01 02 03 04 05 MC 9 8 7 6 5 4 3 2 1

FG

*This is dedicated with love to my mother,
who is a dog person,
and who has endured with grace my
lifelong infatuation with cats.*

*And to Beth Tripmacher and Stephen Lynn,
who worked so hard on this book,
thanks from the bottom of my heart.*

NOTE TO READER

Much effort was expended to find the original sources of the quotations in this book and to quote them correctly. In some cases, the same quote was attributed to multiple sources, so confusion is possible. Dates are included in the Name Index (when they were available) to give context for the quotations. Translations, where they appear, are my own and are subject to the usual interpretive mistakes that are an inescapable part of rendering thought from one language into another. I would love to hear about any corrections, additions, deletions, and suggestions for improvement, and will incorporate them in subsequent printings of this volume. Please write me at the following address:

Denise Little, Tekno-Books
P.O. Box 8296, Green Bay, WI 54308

CATEGORIES

— INTRODUCTION —

Cats always give us something to talk about. That's one of the hallmarks of cat lovers everywhere. Rich or poor, famous or anonymous, when cat people get together, they talk about their cats—sharing tales of their bravery, their cunning, their affection, their exasperating bad habits, their instincts and intelligence, their quirks, their charm. Writers write about cats they've met and invent cat characters for their stories; celebrities tell stories about their pets in interviews; ordinary people everywhere swap cat stories over lunch. Even cat haters aren't exempt— they, too, spend much time and effort talking and writing about cats, perhaps in self-defense.

Because so much has been said and written about our feline friends, there is an exceptional amount of first-rate poetry, literature, and commentary about them, which has resulted in a vast cornucopia of quotations featuring cats. Mark Twain was a great admirer, and his daughter was once quoted as saying, "My mother likes morals, my father likes cats." The French writer Colette had much to say on the subject; in fact, she seems to have preferred cats to people. In works by everyone from Ralph Waldo Emerson to Erma Bombeck, cats are likely to pop up just about anywhere that humans have put words on paper.

The quotes in this book pay tribute to every aspect of the cats we love—the happy lap ornament, the crafty manipulator, the superb athlete, and the fierce hunter. And because cats have left paw prints (and, yes, a few claw marks as well) on every aspect

of human life, scattered throughout are nuggets of
cat facts and explanations of cat-inspired sayings,
including a surprising number of idioms featuring
our four-footed friends—from "cat got your tongue"
to "look what the cat dragged in."

   The Quotable Cat is "purr"fect reading for cat
lovers everywhere. Read and enjoy—and while
you're at it, read a bit to your cats. Let them know
how much they're appreciated, 'cause when it
comes to cats, you can never say enough!

—Denise Little
2000

The "Purr-fect" Cat

There are no ordinary cats.

—COLETTE

I believe cats to be spirits come to earth.
A cat, I am sure, could walk on a cloud
without coming through.
— JULES VERNE

Life would not be worth living without a cat.
— PEGGY BACON

My cat good.
— KOKO,
*female gorilla, in sign language,
about her pet kitten.*

In the beginning, God created man, but seeing him so feeble, He gave him the cat.
— WARREN ECKSTEIN

I've met many thinkers and many cats, but the wisdom of cats is infinitely superior.
— HIPPOLYTE TAINE

Of all God's creatures, there is only one that cannot be made the slave of the lash. That one is the cat. If man could be crossed with a cat it would improve man, but it would deteriorate the cat.
— MARK TWAIN

The cat has too much spirit to have no heart.
— ERNEST MENAUL

It is impossible for a lover of cats to banish
these alert, gentle, and discriminating little friends,
who give us just enough of their regard and com-
plaisance to make us hunger for more.
— AGNES REPPLIER

I like little pussy, her coat is so warm;
And if I don't hurt her, she'll do me no harm.
So I'll not pull her tail, nor drive her away,
But pussy and I very gently will play.
She'll sit by my side, and I'll give her some food,
And she'll love me because I am gentle and good.
— JANE TAYLOR

It has been the providence of Nature to give this creature nine lives instead of one.

— PILPAY

(Oriental fabulist also known as Bidpai)

CAT PAUSE

Nine lives — *The superstition that a cat has nine lives was originally mentioned in the writings of the ancient Indian fabulist Pilpay (or Bidpai), who wrote in Sanskrit millennia ago. The concept's entry into European slang is probably a leftover from the early days of witch-burning. Witches were reputed to be able to take over their cat familiars' bodies nine times. This later was transformed into the "nine lives" of a cat.*

In life there
are two
compensations —
Prozac and cats.

— BRIAN WALSH

Unlike us, cats never outgrow their delight
in cat capacities, nor do they settle finally for
limitations. Cats, I think, live out their lives
fulfilling their expectations.
—IRVING TOWNSEND

Cats are notoriously sore losers. Coming in second
best, especially to someone as poorly coordinated
as a human being, grates their sensibility.
—STEPHEN BAKER

I love cats because I enjoy my home; and little
by little, they become its visible soul.
—JEAN COCTEAU

There are few things in life more heartwarming
than to be welcomed by a cat.
— TAY HOHOFF

Sphinx of my quiet hearth! Who deignst to dwell,
Friend of my toil, companion of mine ease,
Thine is the lore of Ra and Ramses.
— ROSAMUND MARRIOTT WATSON

A cat improves the garden wall in sunshine, and
the hearth in foul weather.
— JUDITH MERKLE RILEY

A home without a cat, and a well-fed, well-petted and properly revered cat, may be a perfect home, perhaps, but how can it prove its title?

—MARK TWAIN

There are two means of refuge from the miseries of life: music and cats.

—ALBERT SCHWEITZER

What greater gift than the love of a cat?

—CHARLES DICKENS

Cats always know whether people like or dislike them. They do not always care to do anything about it.

— WINIFRED CARRIÈRE

CAT PAUSE

Faster than a cat can lick its ear — *This is a trick phrase, meaning "never." A cat can't lick its ear.*

A cat has absolute emotional honesty: human beings, for one reason or another, may hide their feelings, but a cat does not.

— ERNEST HEMINGWAY

Sometimes the veil between human and animal
intelligence wears very thin—then one experiences
the supreme thrill of keeping a cat, or perhaps
allowing oneself to be owned by a cat.
— CATHERINE MANLEY

There is, indeed, no single quality of the cat that
man could not emulate to his advantage.
— CARL VAN VECHTEN

As anyone who has ever been around a cat for any
length of time well knows, cats have enormous
patience with the limitations of the human mind.
— CLEVELAND AMORY

Cat lovers can readily be identified. Their clothes always look old and well used. Their sheets look like bath towels, and their bath towels look like a collection of knitting mistakes.

— ERIC GURNEY

Two cats can live as cheaply as one, and their owner has twice as much fun.

— LLOYD ALEXANDER

CAT NIP

To smile at your cat, relax your face, smile slightly, and slowly blink your eyes. In many cases, if your cat is happy, it will return the smile in the same way.

Cats invented self-esteem; there is not an insecure
bone in their bodies.
— ERMA BOMBECK

I suspect that many an ailurophobe hates cats only
because he feels that they are better than he is —
more honest, more secure, more loved, more
whatever he is not.
— WINIFRED CARRIÈRE

People with insufficient personalities are fond of
cats. These people adore being ignored.
— HENRY MORGAN

I wish I could write as mysterious as a cat.
—EDGAR ALLAN POE

The affinity of writers for cats is something that
has never been satisfactorily explained.
—WILLIAM H. A. CARR

Authors like cats because they are such quiet,
lovable, wise creatures, and cats like authors for
the same reasons.
—ROBERTSON DAVIES

O bard-like spirit! Beautiful
  and swift!
Sweet lover of the pale night:
The dazzling glory of the
  gold-tinged tail,
Thy whisker waving lips!

— PERCY BYSSHE SHELLEY

Which is more beautiful — feline
movement or feline stillness?

— ELIZABETH HAMILTON

As to sagacity, I should say that his judgment respecting the warmest place and the softest cushion in a room is infallible, his punctuality at meal times is admirable, and his pertinacity in jumping on people's shoulders till they give him some of the best of what is going on, indicates great firmness.

—THOMAS HENRY HUXLEY

A cat's rage is beautiful, burning with pure cat flame, all its hair standing up and crackling blue sparks, eyes blazing and sputtering.

—WILLIAM S. BURROUGHS

If a fish is the movement of water embodied,
given shape, then a cat is the diagram and pattern
of subtle air.

— DORIS LESSING

Cats are autocrats of naked self-interest. They are
both amoral and immoral, consciously breaking
rules. Their "evil" look at such times is no human
projection: the cat may be the only animal who
savors the perverse and reflects upon it.

— CAMILLE PAGLIA

For he is a mixture of gravity and waggery.
For he knows that God is his Saviour.
For there is nothing sweeter than his peace
   when at rest.
For there is nothing brisker than his life
   when in motion.
                    —CHRISTOPHER SMART

A cat pours his body on the floor like water.
It is restful just to see him.
                    —WILLIAM LYON PHELPS

The smallest feline is a masterpiece.
　　　　—LEONARDO DA VINCI

To respect the cat is the beginning of the
aesthetic sense.
　　　　—ERASMUS DARWIN

There's no need for a piece of sculpture in a
home that has a cat.
　　　　—WESLEY BATES

If animals could speak, the dog would be a blun-
dering outspoken fellow, but the cat would have
the rare grace of never saying a word too much.
　　　　—MARK TWAIN

All your wondrous wealth of hair;
Dark and fair,
Silken-shaggy, soft and bright
As the clouds and beams of night,
Pays my reverent hand's caress
Back with a friendlier gentleness.

— Algernon Charles Swinburne

Even the
stupidest cat
seems to
know more
than any dog.

— ELEANOR CLARK

The cat is cryptic, and close to strange things
which men cannot see.
— H. P. LOVECRAFT

The greater cats with golden eyes
Stare out between the bars.
— VICTORIA SACKVILLE-WEST

CAT NIP

*Most white blue-eyed cats are deaf. If they have only one
blue eye (some breeds have odd-eyed variants), they'll be
deaf only in the ear on the same side as the blue eye.*

The really great thing about cats
is their endless variety. One can
pick a cat to fit almost any kind
of décor, color scheme, income,
personality, mood. But under
that fur, whatever color it may be,
there still lies, essentially
unchanged, one of the world's
free souls.

— ERIC GURNEY

Many people love cats. From time to time, newspapers print stories about some elderly widow who died and left her entire estate, valued at $3,200,000, to her cat, Fluffkins. Cats read these stories, too, and are always plotting to get named as beneficiaries in their owners' wills. Did you ever wonder where your cat goes when it wanders off for several hours? It meets with other cats in estate-planning seminars. I just thought you should know.

—DAVE BARRY

Cats know how to obtain food without labor, shelter without confinement, and love without penalties.

—W. L. GEORGE

It is easy to understand why the rabble dislike cats. A cat is beautiful; it suggests ideas of luxury, cleanliness, voluptuous pleasures.
—CHARLES BAUDELAIRE

It's too dangerous a journey to risk the cat's life.
—CHARLES LINDBERGH,
refusing to take his cat Pansy on his 1927 trans-Atlantic flight.

There is nothing in the animal world, to my mind, more delightful than grown cats at play. They are so swift and light and graceful, so subtle and designing, and yet so richly comic.
—MONICA EDWARDS

I saw the most beautiful cat today. It was sitting by the side of the road, its two front feet neatly and graciously together. Then it gravely swished around its tail to completely encircle itself. It was so fit and beautifully neat, that gesture, and so self-satisfied, so complacent.

—ANNE SPENCER MORROW LINDBERGH

Time spent with cats is never wasted.

—COLETTE

A dog, I have always said, is prose; a cat is a poem.

—JEAN BURDEN

When it comes to the advantages of cats versus dogs as pets, there is no competition. Try going away for a weekend, leaving your German Shepherd alone with a bowl of dry food, some water, and a litter box.
— ROBERT STEARNS

CAT PAUSE

Raining cats and dogs — *The phrase has several possible roots. The oldest dates back to Norse mythology when Odin was associated with dogs and rain, and witches were associated with cats and storms. Another possible origin is that the bodies of feral dogs and cats would wash into the sewers after a severe rainstorm, piling up in large masses, leading the citizenry to believe it actually had been raining cats and dogs.*

The Owl and the Pussy-cat went to sea
      In a beautiful pea-green boat,
They took some honey and plenty of money,
      Wrapped up in a five pound note.
The Owl looked up to the stars above,
      And sang to a small guitar,
"O lovely Pussy, O Pussy, my love,
      What a beautiful Pussy you are,
          You are,
          You are!
      What a beautiful Pussy you are!"
            —EDWARD LEAR

Cats are smarter than dogs. You can't get eight cats to pull a sled through the snow.
— JEFF VALDEZ

Come, my fine cat, against my warm heart,
Sheathe your sharp claws and settle.
And let my eyes into yours dart,
Where agate sparks with metal.
— CHARLES BAUDELAIRE

I have found my love of cats most helpful in understanding women.
— JOHN SIMON

THOU ART THE GREAT CAT,
THE AVENGER OF THE GODS,
AND THE JUDGE OF WORDS,
AND THE PRESIDENT OF
THE SOVEREIGN CHIEFS AND
THE GOVERNOR OF THE HOLY CIRCLE;
THOU ART INDEED . . .
THE GREAT CAT.
—Inscription on the Royal Tombs
of the XIX and XX Dynasties at
Thebes in Egypt

CAT NIP

*When a cat died in ancient Egypt, its human family
went into full formal mourning, just as they would
have if a human member had died.*

The
Cat's
Meow

Meow is like aloha— it can mean anything.

—HANK KETCHUM

He seems the incarnation of everything soft and silky and velvety, without a sharp edge in his composition, a dreamer whose philosophy is sleep and let sleep.

—SAKI

Cats are rather delicate creatures and they are subject to a good many different ailments, but I have never heard of one who suffered from insomnia.

—JOSEPH WOOD KRUTCH

One reason we admire cats is for their proficiency in one-upmanship. They always seem to come out on top, no matter what they are doing.

—BARBARA WEBSTER

The cat does not offer services. The cat offers itself. Of course he wants care and shelter. You don't buy love for nothing. Like all pure creatures, cats are practical.

—WILLIAM S. BURROUGHS

If there is one spot of sun spilling onto the floor, a cat will find it and soak it up.

—JEAN ASPER MCINTOSH

Are cats lazy? Well, more power to them if they are. Which one of us has not entertained the dream of doing just as he likes, when and how he likes, and as much as he likes?

—FERNAND MÉRY

CAT PAUSE

Nimble as a cat on a hot stove— *In a great hurry to get away. In ancient times, villages had large communal ovens. Inside them were great stone slabs on which bread and oatcakes were baked. Curious cats would leap in to investigate and leap out again at high speed and high volume.*

Cats are connoisseurs of comfort.

—JAMES HERRIOT

Most cats, when they are Out
want to be In, and vice versa,
and often simultaneously.

—LOUIS F. CAMUTI, DVM

Cats can be cooperative when something feels good, which, to a cat, is the way everything is supposed to feel as much of the time as possible.
　　　　　—ROGER A. CARAS

Ignorant people think it's the noise which fighting cats make that is so aggravating, but it ain't so; it's the sickening grammar they use.
　　　　　—MARK TWAIN

Two little kittens, one stormy night,
Began to quarrel, and then to fight;
One had a mouse, the other had none,
And that's the way the quarrel begun.
　　　　　—JANE TAYLOR

A good cat deserves a good rat.
— FRENCH PROVERB

It is, of course, totally pointless to call a cat
when it is intent on the chase. They are deaf
to the interruptive nonsense of humans. They
are on cat business, totally serious and involved.
— JOHN D. MACDONALD

When I play with my cat, who knows whether I
do not make her more sport than she makes me?
— MICHEL DE MONTAIGNE

I have noticed that what cats most appreciate in a human being is not the ability to produce food, which they take for granted—but his or her entertainment value.

—GEOFFREY HOUSEHOLD

 CAT NIP
Of all kinds of cats, only the domestic house cat can carry its tail in a vertical position.

Mr. Cat knows that a whisker spied is not a whole mouse.

—MARGUERITE HENRY

Of all the toys available, none is better designed than the owner himself. A large multipurpose plaything, its parts can be made to move in almost any direction. It comes completely assembled, and it makes a sound when you jump on it.

—Stephen Baker

"It's alright, mate," he said. "It's just Smutty's [the cat's] sense of humor. Whenever anybody sleeps in this room he likes to get up on that beam up there, and just as you're dropping off and all's right with the world, leap onto your stomach."

—Frank Legg

Nothing attracts pawprints to an automobile faster than a fresh wax job or a warm hood.

—Niki Anderson

Cats don't
like change
without
their consent.

—ROGER A. CARAS

A plate is distasteful to a cat, a newspaper still worse. They like to eat sticky pieces of meat sitting on a cushioned chair or a nice Persian rug.

— MARGARET BENSON

CAT PAUSE

Be a cat's paw — *To be the tool of another, the medium of doing another's dirty work. The allusion is to Aesop's fable about the monkey who wanted to get some roasted chestnuts from the fire, and convinced a cat to paw them from the hot ashes. The monkey got the chestnuts, but the cat only got burned paws.*

Fain would the cat fish eat,
But she's loath to wet her feet.

— THOMAS FULLER

At dinner time he would sit in a corner,
concentrating, and suddenly they would say,
"Time to feed the cat," as if it were their own idea.
— LILIAN JACKSON BRAUN

No amount of time can erase the memory of a good
cat, and no amount of masking tape can ever totally
remove his fur from your couch.
— LEO DWORKEN

A catless writer is almost inconceivable. It's a
perverse taste, really, since it would be easier to
write with a herd of buffalo in the room than even
one cat; they make nests in the notes and bite the
end of the pen and walk on the typewriter keys.
— BARBARA HOLLAND

A computer and a cat are somewhat alike — they both purr, and liked to be stroked, and spend a lot of the day motionless. They also have secrets they don't necessarily share.
—JOHN UPDIKE

Cats sleep everywhere on the shelves like motorized bookends.
—AUDREY THOMAS

CAT NIP

The act of petting a cat has been clinically proven to reduce blood pressure in humans.

You cannot look at a sleeping
cat and feel tense.

—JANE PAULEY

The ideal of calm exists in
a sitting cat.

—JULES RENARD

Cats will always lie soft.

—THEOCRITUS

He's like a cat; fling him which way you will, he'll
light on his legs.
—JOHN RAY

—But the Kitten, how she starts,
Crouches, stretches, paws, and darts!
—WILLIAM WORDSWORTH

Do you see that kitten chasing so prettily her own
tail? If you could look with her eyes, you might
see her surrounded with hundreds of figures
performing complex dramas, with tragic and comic
issues, long conversations, many characters, many
ups and downs of fate.
—RALPH WALDO EMERSON

There is no more intrepid explorer than a kitten.
— JULES CHAMPFLEURY

A kitten is chiefly remarkable for rushing about like mad at nothing whatever, and generally stopping before it gets there.
— AGNES REPPLIER

An ordinary kitten will ask more questions than any five year old.
— CARL VAN VECHTEN

Those who'll play with cats must expect to be scratched.
— MIGUEL DE CERVANTES

The more you rub a cat on the rump, the higher she sets her tail.
> —JOHN RAY

The cat could both arch its back and purr. Oh yes, it could also make sparks if you rubbed its fur the wrong way.
> —HANS CHRISTIAN ANDERSEN

CAT PAUSE

Don't get your back up!— *Meaning don't get upset or angry. This is a reference to the way a cat reacts when riled, by arching its back and spitting.*

My cats have fleas. This worries me, but not for the reasons you'd think. The cats never leave the apartment. The only one going in and out is me. That means they have to be getting their fleas from ME!

—PAULA POUNDSTONE

I found out why cats drink out of the toilet. My mother told me it's because the water is cold in there. And I'm like: How did my mother know THAT?

—WENDY LIEBMAN

A lame cat is better than a swift horse when rats infest the palace.

—CHINESE PROVERB

The clever cat eats cheese and breathes down
rat holes with baited breath.
    —W. C. FIELDS

A cat's idea of a "good time" is to kill something.
    —ANDY ROONEY

CAT NIP

*Every attempt to make a mouse-flavored cat food has
been rejected by cats when tested on them.*

I don't think it is so much the actual bath that most
cats dislike; I think it's the fact that they have to
spend a good part of the day putting their hair
back in place.

— DEBBIE PETERSON

Just as the would-be debutante will fret and fuss
over every detail till all is perfect, so will the
fastidious feline patiently toil until every whiskertip
is in place.

— LYNN HOLLYN

Cats are the ultimate narcissists. You can tell this because of all the time they spend on personal grooming. Dogs aren't like this. A dog's idea of personal grooming is to roll in a dead fish.

—JAMES GORMAN

All you have to remember is Rule 1:
When in doubt—Wash.

—PAUL GALLICO

CAT NIP
Cats spend nearly half of their waking hours grooming themselves.

Dame Trot and her cat
Sat down for to chat;
The Dame sat on this side,
And Puss sat on that.
"Puss," says the Dame,
"Can you catch a rat,
Or a mouse in the dark?"
"Purr," says the cat.

—TRADITIONAL NURSERY RHYME

The Whole "Kitten" Kaboodle

Cats are intended to teach us that not everything in nature has a purpose.

—GARRISON KEILLOR

One cat just leads to another.
—ERNEST HEMINGWAY

Cat: an alarm clock with claws and no
snooze button.
—DENISE LITTLE

CAT PAUSE

Look what the cat dragged in — *To be bedraggled
and much the worse for wear. This is an expression
resulting from the general state of anything a cat brings
into the house. These items, often intended as presents
for much-loved owners, are usually traumatized or
dead prey animals, and their appearance reflects it.*

I have a little pussy
And her coat is silver-grey;
She lives in the meadow
And she never runs away.
She'll always be a pussy,
She'll never be a cat,
Because — she's a pussy willow!
Now what do you think of that?

—TRADITIONAL NURSERY RHYME

Always the cat remains a little beyond the limits
we try to set for him in our blind folly.
—ANDRE NORTON

The mathematical probability of a common
cat doing exactly as it pleases is the one
scientific absolute in the world.
—LYNN M. OSBAND

Any normal, ordinary cat can keep any human
being in a state of frustration.
—GLADYS TABOR

Some people say that cats are sneaky, evil, and cruel. True, and they have many other fine qualities as well.

—MISSY DIZICK AND MARY BLY

The great charm of cats is their rampant egotism,
their devil-may-care attitude toward responsibility,
their disinclination to earn an honest dollar.
—ROBERTSON DAVIES

A Cat caught a Cock, and pondered how he
might find a reasonable excuse to eat him.
He called the Cock a nuisance to men who crowed
in the dark of morning and woke them up.
The Cock said he did this for men's benefit,
that they might rise in time for their work.
The Cat replied "Although you abound in specious
apologies, I shall not remain supperless," and
dined lavishly. The moral: The Cat does as
the Cat will—and any excuse will serve.
—AESOP

When my cats aren't happy, I'm not happy.
Not because I care about their mood but because
I know they're just sitting there thinking up
ways to get even.
— PENNY WARD MOSER

The wildcat is the "real" cat, the soul of the
domestic cat; unknowable to human beings, he
exists inside our household pets, who long ago have
seduced us with their seemingly civilized ways.
— JOYCE CAROL OATES

When she walked…she stretched out long and thin
like a little tiger, and held her head high to look over
the grass as if she were treading the jungle.
— SARAH ORNE JEWETT

God made the cat in order that man might have
the pleasure of caressing the tiger.
—FERNAND MÉRY

Prowling his own quiet backyard or asleep by the
fire, he is still only a whisker away from the wilds.
—JEAN BURDEN

CAT PAUSE

Not a cat's chance in hell— *This phrase is confusing,
but only because the root phrase has been lost. The
original phrase was "not a cat's chance in hell without
claws," pointing out the risks of taking on a serious
enemy without proper weapons.*

I had been told that the training procedure with
cats was difficult. It's not. Mine had me trained
in two days.

—BILL DANA

Our old cat has kittens three
And I fancy these their names will be:
Pepperpot, Sootikin, Scratchaway—there!
Were ever kittens with these to compare?
And we call the old mother—
        Now what do you think?—
Tabitha Longclaws Tiddley Wink.

—THOMAS HOOD

Women and cats will do as they please, and men and dogs should relax and get used to the idea.

—ROBERT A. HEINLEIN

No matter how much cats fight, there always seem to be plenty of kittens.

—ABRAHAM LINCOLN

A man who was loved by 300 women singled me out to live with him. Why? I was the only one without a cat.

—ELAYNE BOOSLER

Man wishes woman to be peaceable, but in fact she is essentially warlike, like the cat.
— FRIEDRICH NIETZSCHE

I could half persuade myself that the word felonious is derived from the feline temper.
— ROBERT SOUTHEY

We have a theory that cats are planning to take over the world, just try to look them straight in the eye . . . yup, they're hiding something!
— *Dog Fancy*

A dog is like a liberal. He wants to please every-body. A cat really doesn't need to know that everybody loves him.

—WILLIAM KUNSTLER

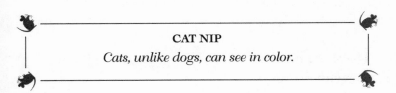

CAT NIP

Cats, unlike dogs, can see in color.

When you command a dog to "sit up," the poor idiot thinks he has to do it. The average cat throws off, pretends to be stupid and not to understand what you want. He really understands you too well, but he sees "nothing in it" for him. Why sit up?

—WILLIAM LYON PHELPS

Sing, sing, what shall I sing?
The cat's run away with the pudding bag string!
Do, do, what shall I do?
The cat has bitten it quite in two.

— TRADITIONAL NURSERY RHYME

There are more ways of killing a cat than choking
her with cream.

— CHARLES KINGSLEY

When the cat's away,
The mice will play.

— JOHN RAY

Cats are dangerous companions for writers because
cat-watching is a near-perfect method of writing
avoidance.
> —DAN GREENBURG

It's funny how dogs and cats know the inside of
folks better than other folks do, isn't it?
> —ELEANOR H. PORTER

A man has to work so hard so that something of
his personality stays alive. A tomcat has it so easy,
he has only to spray and his presence is there for
years on rainy days.
> —ALBERT EINSTEIN

In a cat's eye, all things belong to cats.
— ENGLISH PROVERB

One cat in a household is a sign of loneliness, two of barrenness, and three of sodomy.
— EDWARD DAHLBERG

It would have made a cat laugh.
— J. R. PLANCHÉ

CAT NIP

Spraying an item with a weak mixture of lemon juice and water will discourage a cat from scratching or investigating it. (This will also have a slight bleaching effect, so it works beautifully on houseplants, but probably isn't suitable for your antique sofa.)

There once were two cats from
    Kilkenny.
Each thought there was one cat
    too many.
So they fought and they fit,
And they scratched and they bit
'Til, excepting their nails
And the tips of their tails,
Instead of two cats, there
    weren't any.

— KATHERINE ELEANOR CONWAY

I gave my cat a bath the other day...they love it.
He sat there, he enjoyed it, it was fun for me. The
fur would stick to my tongue, but other than that...
— STEVE MARTIN

To bathe a cat takes brute force, perseverance,
courage of conviction—and a cat. The last ingredi-
ent is usually hardest to come by.
— STEPHEN BAKER

Never try to outstubborn a cat.
— ROBERT A. HEINLEIN

Dogs come when they're called; cats take a
message and get back to you.
— MISSY DIZICK AND MARY BLY

The vanity of man
revolts from
the serene indifference
of the cat.

—AGNES REPPLIER

With the qualities of cleanliness, discretion, affection, patience, dignity, and courage that cats have, how many of us, I ask you, would be capable of being cats?
—FERNAND MÉRY

Cat people are different, to the extent that they generally are not conformists. How could they be, with a cat running their lives?
—LOUIS J. CAMUTI, DVM

In nine lifetimes, you'll never know as much about your cat as your cat knows about you.
—MICHAEL ZULLO

The problem with cats is that
they get the same exact look
whether they see a moth or an
ax-murderer.

— PAULA POUNDSTONE

Confound the cats! All cats — always —
Cats of all colors, black, white, grey;
By night a nuisance and by day —
    Confound the cats!

— ORLANDO DOBBIN

If toast always lands butter-side down, and cats always land on their feet, what happens if you strap toast on the back of a cat and drop it?

—STEVEN WRIGHT

CAT PAUSE

Like a cat on a hot tin roof—*An expression from the American South, co-opted by Tennessee Williams for his play. Tin roofs get too hot to touch under the summer sunlight, and the unlucky cat who decides to jump onto one, seeking a high vantage point to lurk in, invariably gets burned and has to take a quick leap back down to the ground.*

There are people who reshape the world by force or argument, but the cat just lies there, dozing, and the world quietly reshapes itself to suit his comfort and convenience.

— ALLEN AND IVY DODD

If a cat does something, we call it instinct; if we do the same thing, for the same reason, we call it intelligence.

— WILL CUPPY

The way to get on with a cat is to treat it as an equal — or even better, as the superior it knows itself to be.

— ELIZABETH PETERS

The trouble with cats is that they've got no tact.
—P. G. WODEHOUSE

If a cat spoke, it would say things like "Hey, I don't see the *problem* here."
—ROY BLOUNT JR.

CAT PAUSE

Cat got your tongue? — *Meaning "why aren't you speaking?" The phrase is probably ancient middle-Eastern in origin. The traditional punishment for lying in that time and place was having one's tongue cut out. The resulting organs were often later fed to the ruler's pet cats.*

My cat does not talk as respectfully to me
as I do to her.
  —COLETTE

"Goodness me! Why, what was that?"
"Silent be. It was the cat!"
  —W. S. GILBERT

Who's that ringing at my doorbell?
A little pussycat that isn't very well.
Rub its nose with a little mutton fat,
That's the best cure for a little pussy cat.
  —D'ARCY WENTWORTH THOMPSON

The phrase "domestic cat" is an oxymoron.
— GEORGE F. WILL

Comets are like cats. They have tails, and they
do precisely what they want.
— DAVID H. LEVY

The wildest of all wild animals was the Cat. He
walked by himself, and all places were alike to him.
— RUDYARD KIPLING

As every cat owner knows, nobody owns a cat.
— ELLEN PERRY BERKELEY

The cat lives his own life;
he expects you to live yours.

— NELSON ANTRIM CRAWFORD

A cat's got her own opinion of human beings. She don't say much, but you can tell enough to make you anxious not to hear the whole of it.
— JEROME K. JEROME

Who can believe that there is no soul behind those luminous eyes!
— THÉOPHILE GAUTIER

"All right," said the Cat, and this time it vanished quite slowly, beginning with the end of the tail, and ending with the grin, which remained some time after the rest of it had gone.
— LEWIS CARROLL

Oh, the cats in this town have their secrets.
— MARY VIRGINIA MICKA

CAT PAUSE

Let the cat out of the bag — *Meaning "to reveal a secret." This phrase dates back to the old English market practice of putting suckling pigs in cloth bags (called "pokes"—as in "pig in a poke") after they were sold to make it easy for the purchaser to carry them home. Unscrupulous vendors would substitute cats for the pigs, and when the bag was opened, the vendor's secret was made clear.*

If you would know a man, observe how he
treats a cat.

—ROBERT A. HEINLEIN

If we treated everyone we meet with the same
affection we bestow upon our favorite cat, they,
too, would purr.

—MARTIN BUXBAUM

The more people I meet the more I like my cat.

—ANONYMOUS

No tame animal has lost less of its native dignity
or maintained more of its ancient reserve.
The domestic cat might rebel tomorrow.
—WILLIAM CONWAY

Cats seem to go on the principle that it never does
any harm to ask for what you want.
—JOSEPH WOOD KRUTCH

Kittens believe that all nature is occupied with
their diversion.
—F. A. PARADIS DE MONCRIF

Watch a cat when it enters a room for the first time.
It searches and smells about, it is not quiet for a
moment, it trusts nothing until it has examined and
made acquaintance with everything.
— JEAN-JACQUES ROUSSEAU

Who can tell what just speculations Murr the Cat
may be passing on us beings of wider speculation?
— GEORGE ELIOT

It always gives me a shiver when I see a cat seeing
what I can't see.
— ELEANOR FARJEON

I've got a cat, but what good is it?
>—ANTON CHEKHOV

It is difficult to obtain the friendship of a cat. It is a philosophical animal . . . one that does not place its affections thoughtlessly.
>—THÉOPHILE GAUTIER

There is, incidentally, no way of talking about cats that enables one to come off as a sane person.
>—DAN GREENBURG

They say the test of literary power is whether a man can write an inscription. I say, "Can he name a kitten?"

—SAMUEL BUTLER

I and Pangur Ban, my cat,
'Tis a like task we are at;
Hunting mice is his delight,
Hunting words I sit all night.

—UNKNOWN IRISH MONK,
circa eighth century

Cats are selfish. A man waits on a cat hand and foot for weeks, humoring its lightest whim, and then it goes and leaves him flat because it has found a place down the road where the fish are more frequent.
— P. G. WODEHOUSE

Curiosity killed the cat, but for a while I was a suspect.
— STEVEN WRIGHT

CAT NIP

In the wild, cats spend an average of twenty hours of each day sleeping. Domestic cats average about 16 to 18 hours per day of snooze time.

I have a kitten, my dear, the drollest of all
creatures that ever wore a cat's skin. Her gambols
are not to be described and would be incredible
if they could. In point of size she is likely to be a
kitten always, being extremely small for her age,
but time I suppose that spoils everything will
make her also a cat.
— WILLIAM COWPER

As one who has long been a pushover for cats,
I should like to offer a packet of color-fast,
preshrunk advice. If a stray kitten bounds out
of nowhere when you're taking a walk, mews
piteously, and rubs a soft shoulder against your
leg, flee to the hills until the danger is over.
— MURRAY ROBINSON

A dog will often steal a bone,
But Conscience lets him not alone,
And by his tail his guilt is known.
But cats consider theft a game,
And, Howsoever you may blame,
Refuse the slightest sign of shame.
— ANONYMOUS

If you want to be a psychological novelist and
write about human beings, the best thing you
can do is keep a pair of cats.
— ALDOUS HUXLEY

A cat will be your friend, but never your slave.
— THÉOPHILE GAUTIER

If there *is* another way to skin a cat, I don't
want to know about it.
— STEVE KRAVITZ

 CAT PAUSE
There's more than one way to skin a cat —
*Thankfully, this one isn't about cats at all. The reference
is to preparing a catfish (which is called a "cat"-fish
because of its long whiskers) for cooking. The fish must
be skinned because the skin is tough, but there are
multiple ways to go about skinning the fish.*

I am the cat of cats, I am
The everlasting cat!
Cunning, and old, and sleek as jam,
The everlasting cat!
I hunt the vermin in the night—
The everlasting cat!
For I see best without the light—
The everlasting cat!

—WILLIAM BRIGHTLY RANDS

—— NAME INDEX ——

Aesop, circa 570 B. C.
Alexander, Lloyd (1924-)
Amory, Cleveland (1917-1998)
Andersen, Hans Christian (1805-1875)
Anderson, Niki, *What My Cat Has Taught Me About Life*
Bacon, Peggy (1895-1987)
Baker, Stephen (1921-)
Barry, Dave (1947-)
Bates, Wesley (1947-)
Baudelaire, Charles (1821-1867)
Benson, Margaret (1865-1916)
Berkeley, Ellen Perry (1931-)
Blount Jr., Roy (1941-)
Bly, Mary, *Dogs Are Better Than Cats!*
Bombeck, Erma (1927-1996)
Boosler, Elayne (1952-)
Braun, Lilian Jackson (1916?-)
Burden, Jean (1914-)
Burroughs, William S. (1914-1997)
Butler, Samuel (1612-1680)
Buxbaum, Martin (1912-1991)
Camuti, Louis J., DVM (1893-1981)
Caras, Roger A. (1928-)
Carr, William H. A. (1902-)
Carroll, Lewis (Charles Ludwidge Dodgson) (1832-1898)
Carrière, Winifred, *Cats, 24 hours A Day*
Cervantes, Miguel de (1547-1616)

Champfleury, Jules (1821-1889)
Chekhov, Anton (1860-1904)
Clark, Eleanor (1912-1996)
Cocteau, Jean (1889-1963)
Colette (1873-1954)
Conway, Katherine Eleanor (1853-1927)
Conway, William (1894-1983)
Cowper, William (1731-1800)
Crawford, Nelson Antrim (1888-?)
Cuppy, Will (1884-1949)
da Vinci, Leonardo (1452-1519)
Dahlberg, Edward (1900-1977)
Dana, Bill (1924-)
Darwin, Erasmus (1731-1802)
Davies, Robertson (1913-1995)
de Montaigne, Michel (1533-1592)
Dickens, Charles (1812-1870)
Dizick, Missy, *Dogs Are Better Than Cats!*
Dobbin, Orlando (1807-1890)
Dodd, Allen E., and Ivy, *Tale of Two Cats*
Dworken, Leo, *Is Your Dog Jewish?*
Eckstein, Warren, *Illustrated Cat's Life*
Edwards, Monica (1912-1998)
Einstein, Albert (1879-1955)
Eliot, George (Mary Ann Evans Cross) (1819-1880)
Emerson, Ralph Waldo (1803-1882)
Farjeon, Eleanor (1881-1965)
Fields, W. C., (1880-1946)
Fuller, Thomas (1654-1734)
Gallico, Paul (1897-1976)
Gautier, Théophile (1811-1872)
George, W. L., (1882-1926)
Gilbert, W. S. (1836-1911)

Gorman, James (1949-)
Greenburg, Dan (1936-)
Gurney, Eric, *Impossible Dogs and Troublesome Cats*
Hamilton, Elizabeth (1902-)
Heinlein, Robert A., (1907-1988)
Hemingway, Ernest (1899-1961)
Henry, Marguerite (1902-)
Herriot, James (Alf Wight) (1917-1995)
Hohoff, Tay (Therese von Hohoff Torrey) (1898-1974)
Holland, Barbara (1944-)
Hollyn, Lynn, *Lynn Hollyn's Town and Country Cat*
Hood, Thomas (1799-1845)
Household, Geoffrey (1900-1988)
Huxley, Aldous (1894-1963)
Huxley, Thomas Henry (1825-1895)
Jerome, Jerome K., (1859-1927)
Jewett, Sarah Orne (1849-1909)
Keillor, Garrison (1942-)
Ketchum, Hank (1920-)
Kingsley, Charles (1819-1875)
Kipling, Rudyard (1865-1936)
Koko, female gorilla, circa 1981
Kravitz, Steve (1965-)
Krutch, Joseph Wood (1893-1970)
Kunstler, William (1919-1995)
Lear, Edward (1812-1888)
Legg, Frank (1906-1966)
Lessing, Doris (1919-)
Levy, David H. (1948-)
Liebman, Wendy
Lincoln, Abraham (1809-1865)
Lindbergh, Anne Spencer Morrow (1906-)
Lindbergh, Charles (1902-1974)

Little, Denise (1957-)
Lovecraft, H. P., (1890-1937)
MacDonald, John D. (1916-1986)
McIntosh, Jean Asper
Manley, Catherine, *Your Cat or Mine*
Martin, Steve (1945-)
Menaul, Ernest (1830-1903)
Méry, Fernand (1897-1984)
Micka, Mary Virginia (1922-)
Morgan, Henry (1825-1884)
Moser, Penny Ward
Nietzsche, Friedrich (1844-1900)
Norton, Andre (1912-)
Oates, Joyce Carol (1938-)
Osband, Lynn M.
Paglia, Camille (1947-)
Paradis de Moncrif, F. A. (1687-1770)
Pauley, Jane (1950-)
Peters, Elizabeth (Barbara Mertz) (1927-)
Peterson, Debbie (1950-)
Phelps, William Lyon (1865-1943)
Pilpay (Oriental fabulist also known as Bidpai)
Planché, J. R., (1796-1880)
Poe, Edgar Allan (1809-1849)
Porter, Eleanor H. (1868-1920)
Poundstone, Paula (1959-)
Rands, William Brightly (1823-1882)
Ray, John (1628-1705)
Repplier, Agnes (1855-1950)
Renard, Jules (1864-1910)
Riley, Judith Merkle (1942-)
Robinson, Murray, circa 1951
Rooney, Andy (1919-)

Rousseau, Jean-Jacques (1712-1778)
Sackville-West, Victoria (1892-1962)
Saki (H. H. Munro) (1870-1916)
Schweitzer, Albert (1875-1965)
Shelley, Percy Bysshe (1792-1822)
Simon, John (1933-)
Smart, Christopher (1722-1771)
Southey, Robert (1774-1843)
Stearns, Robert (1938-)
Swinburne, Algernon Charles (1837-1909)
Tabor, Gladys (1899-)
Taine, Hippolyte (1828-1893)
Taylor, Jane (1783-1824)
Theocritus (c.310 B.C.-250 B.C.)
Thomas, Audrey (1938-)
Thompson, D'Arcy Wentworth (1829-1902)
Townsend, Irving (1920-1981)
Twain, Mark (Samuel L. Clemens) (1835-1910)
Updike, John (1932-)
Valdez, Jeff
Van Vechten, Carl (1880-1964)
Verne, Jules (1828-1905)
Walsh, Brian (1953-)
Watson, Rosamund Marriott (1863-1911)
Webster, Barbara (1900-)
Will, George F. (1941-)
Wodehouse, P. G. (1881-1975)
Wordsworth, William (1770-1850)
Wright, Steven (1965-)
Zullo, Michael, *Cat Astrology*